Beyond
the Velvet
Curtain

Wick Poetry First Book Series
Maggie Anderson, Editor

Already the World
Victoria Redel   Gerald Stern, Judge

Likely
Lisa Coffman   Alicia Suskin Ostriker, Judge

Intended Place
Rosemary Willey   Yusef Komunyakaa, Judge

The Apprentice of Fever
Richard Tayson   Marilyn Hacker, Judge

Beyond the Velvet Curtain
Karen Kovacik   Henry Taylor, Judge

Beyond
the Velvet
Curtain

Poems by

Karen Kovacik

For Jamie's
with wishes
for many more et [?]
in the "science & compassion"
and [?]."

Karen Kovacik

7/15/05
Cleveland

The Kent State University Press
Kent, Ohio, and London, England

© 1999 by Karen Kovacik
All rights reserved
Library of Congress Catalog Card Number 99-22463
ISBN 0-87338-646-9 (cloth)
ISBN 0-87338-647-7 (pbk.)
Manufactured in the United States of America

06 05 04 03 02 01 00 99   5 4 3 2 1

The Wick First Book Series is sponsored by the Stan and Tom Wick Poetry
Program and the Department of English at Kent State University.

Kovacik, Karen, 1959–
        Beyond the velvet curtain: poems / by Karen Kovacik.
            p.   cm. — (Wick poetry first book series)
        ISBN 0-87338-646-9 (cloth: alk. paper) ∞
        ISBN 0-87338-647-7 (pbk.: alk. paper) ∞
        I. Title.   II. Series.
        PS3561.O854B49   1999   99-22463
        811'.54 — dc21

British Library Cataloging-in-Publication data are available.

for Marilyn Annucci

for Eric Swank

Contents

IV Exile

Acknowledgments

I would like to acknowledge with gratitude the magazines in which these poems first appeared, some in earlier versions: "During the Sorties over Baghdad," "Polish Jokes," *Artful Dodge;* "Wedding Song," *Beloit Poetry Journal;* "Losing Language," *Black Swan Review;* "The Art of Love," "Come as You Are," *The Cape Rock;* "Drought," *Cincinnati Poetry Review;* "As My Husband Translates from the Polish," *Confrontation;* "Käthe Kollwitz, after a Visit to the New Russia, 1927," *Emrys Journal;* "Miss Victory (1895)," *Gulf Coast;* "Revising Sylvia," *The Journal;* "Hermann Kafka's Dinnertime Pantoum," *Lake Effect;* "Breslau," *Laurel Review;* "Nixon and Nikita in the Kitchen," "Nixon on the Pleasures of Undressing a Woman," "Pat Nixon Speaks of Her Husband's Snoring," "Sapphic Sonnets" (*Z, S, M*), *Madison Review;* "Learning to Draw," *Mississippi Valley Review;* "Einstein's Train," *New Virginia Review;* "Exile," *Poets On;* "Watching My Father Pray," *Rafters;* "Citoyen," "Dust Devils," "WCW on Marsden Hartley," *Salmagundi;* and "Saint Elizabeth, Queen of Hungary," *SAM* (School of the Art Institute of Chicago).

Generous support from the University of Wisconsin Institute for Creative Writing and the Ohio Arts Council helped with the preparation of this book.

"Cuba Libre" owes a great debt, of course, to Elizabeth Bishop's "In the Waiting Room."

A big spasibo to Maggie Anderson, Marilyn Annucci, Daniel Bourne, Christine Brooks, David Citino, Alice Cone, Ellen Damsky, Ceci Gray, Susan Grimm, Alice Fulton, Erin Holman, Jesse Lee Kercheval, Stacy Klein, Linda Kovacik, Jeredith Merrin, Ruth L. Schwartz, Ellen Seusy, Songofemi, Eric Swank, Leonard Trawick, Alberta Turner, and Ron Wallace.

And to Henry Taylor, thanks for noticing.

Foreword by Henry Taylor

In the presence of certain kinds of excellence in poetry, there is the temptation to say that they speak for some enduring principles of the art. This book makes me want to say, as I have said before and will again, that play—pure high spirits in the skilled and sensitive arrangement of words and parts of words—may be what helps a poet most when the poet is concerned both with engaging emotion and avoiding sentimentality.

The book's four sections are titled with appropriate abstractions, though the word "Statecraft" takes on hilarious overtones as we become acquainted with this particular version of a late former president, or someone with his name and a few of his attributes. In fact, it is the obvious gulf between this character and the one in our memories that makes some of these poems so magically, impossibly plausible. "Nixon on the Pleasures of Undressing a Woman" opens with a reasonable assertion: "With us, it is easy: a tug on the tie, the ubiquitous zipper." Maybe so. But recall for a moment, as this poem seems tacitly to invite us to do, the incredible awkwardness of the actual Nixon walking on the beach in a business suit. At such a moment he gave the impression that he could never get undressed. Yet here is the speaker lingering "in Pat's closet" and being reminded of his Russian stacking dolls. A few pages further on, Krushchev finds him "diminutive and charming." These may not be the very last adjectives I would think to apply to the actual Nixon, but they're close enough. This is a brilliant sequence, and it is a bold stroke to open a book with something so distinctive, so nearly self-contained, and so hard, one might think, to follow.

The title of the second section, "Mastery," is a word that women tend to use thoughtfully—as indeed Ms. Kovacik does here. The various situations of some of these poems—learning to draw and paint, taking on the voice of William Carlos Williams, or of Käthe Kollwitz—combine with the force of the Nixon sequence to keep the reader suspended above the question of who the "I" might be in some of the apparently more personal poems, such as "Dust Devils" and "As My Husband Translates from the Polish." The collection is by now well in to its serious work of blurring the distinction some readers like to draw between actual and imagined experience.

The acquisition of skill is a form of mastery, and someone in the third section is learning various domestic skills but is also aware of the risk of being mastered. The section opens with another flamboyantly imaginative treatment of a character with the same name as someone who actually lived: "Hermann Kafka's Dinnertime Pantoum" is a superb achievement, not only for the steadiness with which it manages its loony invention ("Manners, for a Kafka, are everything"), but also because it comes brilliantly along at a moment when it might be about time to give the pantoum a rest for a while, along with the unmetrical sestina and the word "pentimento." Ms. Kovacik appears to be most at ease in risky territory; she cheerfully assembles at the end of the section a series of poems partly concerned with modes of sexuality various enough to raise once more the question of how many characters are involved here.

Throughout the second and third sections, there have been reference to Polish forebears, and "Exile" brings into sharper focus some of the outlines those references suggest. The title poem is a moving address to dead forebears with whom the speaker finds she has much in common. There are several other quite powerful poems of loss and remembrance here, but even in their midst, Ms. Kovacik has the tact to drop something like the surprising sonnet, "Lawrence Welk." The pleasures of that poem are somewhat like those of thinking about the difference between the Nixon I used to think I knew and the one Ms. Kovacik has constructed, since it ends with a character wishing there were no boundaries between the television show and the living room.

We make the worlds we live in as best we can, out of the materials we have been given. The worlds of *Beyond the Velvet Curtain* are in some ways remote from mine, but like mine, they run on good will and a faith in the power of human love. I am grateful to have encountered these poems.

The purpose of poetry is to remind us
how difficult it is to remain just one person,
for our house is open, there are no keys in the doors,
and invisible guests come in and out at will.

—Czesław Miłosz, "Ars poetica?"

Beyond
the Velvet
Curtain

I
Statecraft

Nixon on the Pleasures of Undressing a Woman

With us, it is easy: a tug on the tie, the ubiquitous zipper.
But with a woman, you can never be certain how deep
the layers go. First, perhaps, a jacket of mink, gloves

lapping up the greedy length of the arm, shoes
like airy Eiffels for the feet. Then the untethering
of beads and bracelets, the slow dismantling

of those hanging gardens of skirt
crashing around foundations of lace and bone.
And right when the patience has died in your fingers,

and your tongue has gone cool and dry with desire,
you are suddenly faced with that blinding symmetry
both spherical and isosceles, the twin raptures

of Sinai and Everest. Some mornings I linger
in Pat's closet, among all the incompatible species
of fox and alligator, ostrich and lamb.

And I'm reminded of my Russian stacking dolls:
how the smallest is absolutely empty
but for silence, longing, a residue of perfume.

Pat Nixon Speaks of Her Husband's Snoring

San Clemente, 1975

For all I know his communiqués
animate the gray Pacific or ascend
to Andromeda and beyond,
where perhaps they are monitored
by some perplexed citizen of the universe.

Most nights I have to draw away from the sound
the way Moses withdrew from the burning bush.
That it is human nature to avoid the sources of things
the waking Dick will readily admit, but when he sleeps
he is no longer a slump-shouldered ex-president

in pajamas, but a chieftain, a prophet
who wishes to coax into his flock
even the reluctant redwoods, the mute
cliffs of rock along the coast, and the ocean
with its everlasting in and out.

Citoyen

"Oh missionary, oh honey," I say
as you shift me onto my back, still
inside me. You are all agility
and thrift. Robespierre didn't spill

a drop of wine that was the Revolution's.
And in your full-hipped embrace, my darling,
I am the Third Estate, I am rising
and you are Robespierre making love

with a peasant who beat up her neighbor
for bread last Tuesday. Hunger makes us
desperate. I see it in your white
Canadian cheekbones, the cool flares

of your eyes, your thick
scarred fingers so unlike a scholar's.
I am disgusted by the bourgeoise in me
who wants to seat you by the oilcloth

and serve you roast beef and wine,
good bread and potatoes. But I wait on you,
I wait. For weeks I have stalked you
and now that I have you in my kitchen

I am shy, I am patient, putting
you to work with knife and cutting board,
insisting on a certain width of celery.
How to convey to you that it is not just your body

without clothes I am after. Not just your white
hips, your black hair. But everything else:
your manic brother sprinkling holy water
on the dogs of the neighborhood, the hearth

your family built of stones from Sunday walks,
the vacant priest you become after days without sleep
or food. Despite everything, you are pure
and I hate you for it. I request

that we leave the lights on, and it's so good,
so much like sin, our hipbones shifting like stones.
We begin the slow march on the capital, we beat
the slow sheep home.

Nixon's Nightmare

The White House, June 1974

B-52s with heavy payloads whinny
over the reflecting pools at Versailles.
The co-pilot lines up the crosshairs
over a slender tower and swollen dome,
then a mansion packed with antiques.

The Rose Garden erupts, President Lincolns
and American Beauties roused
from their beds. Century-old oaks shudder
and surrender. The head of state
deserts his burning house, dives

into a pool, his powdered wig, a limp relic,
bobbing on the surface. *Après moi*, he gasps,
le déluge. Nearby, a traitor in spectacles
untwists the pin of a grenade. Serpents
of reel-to-reel shoot through the pool.

Breslau

In its eight hundred years of existence, the Silesian city of Breslau (in Polish, Wrocław) changed hands several times—belonging to Poland, to Prussia, and later, to Germany, and now again to Poland. In this poem, a German archaeology student from Breslau, though disgusted by Nazi propaganda that mythologizes the German past, becomes obsessed with preserving ordinary artifacts of daily life in the city. Ironically, after the war, when Breslau is again converted into Wrocław, most traces of its German past are obliterated.

1939
I see everything in layers:
trees, cities, species, the sexuality
of the boy who shares my desk.
Sap rings, slivers of terra cotta, fossilized
insects with horned teeth, Marlene Dietrich in black
stockings and garter belt, Marlene sucking on
a long cigarette, spongy Marlene tissue
that summons blood to the penis.

Now I slouch against the pillows
like an invalid. From the balcony opposite
I hear trumpets pointed
toward the distant Reichstag, toward the gaudy
Victory Angel whose wingspan is broad
as a Luftwaffe bomber's. When
the loudspeakers first crackle with references
to ancient Rome, I can already picture
the enormous central mass
of the *Jahrhunderthalle*
crumbling into lacy ruin
like the great Colosseum.

1945
A hairless kitten licks my leg. Sometimes
I kick it to stop its senseless
Mühe, Mühe. I leave my bed only
after dark. By night, under the blacked out
starless sky, I bury things so people will know
the Breslau of my childhood. By day,
I catalog everything in this room.
Not just *saucer* and *transom*
but the way the rounded bottoms
of teacups fit, the thick aroma of coal wafting in.
Not just my mother's *eyeglasses* but the tiny scrolls
of nacre along the bridge. Not just *featherbed*
but the boy who kissed me over and over
in Hungarian.

Breslau these days is both a mineshaft
and the men trapped in it. All around
I hear a strangle of voices
as the lamps snuff out, the walls
crumble in, the canaries
leave off singing.

The Philosopher Nixon at Frisbee

It began as a game with his grandkids, an absurd pursuit
and drift on the grass, in the shrubs,
his slacks stained at the knee, his dress shirt ringed with sweat—
so unlike the thinking man's sport of poker,
in which eye and hand do their rapacious deed
with grace. How easy the bluff and bid
compared to this lawn democracy.

"Make your fingers into a peace sign, Grandpa,"
the twelve-year-old says, demonstrating how to sail
the saucer low and steady rather than curving it
back like a staircase. How true the maxim
about the bird in hand. Things in flight *are* unseizable
as power. Nixon wishes he could poise forever

at the lip of intention, at the slow moment
before execution, when the body, tensed and ready,
feels incapable of awkwardness or error.
He imagines himself oiled and nude,
wearing the wreath of stamina and ease,
his body not the aimless arrow
but the tightened bow.

Miss Victory (1895)

Monument Circle, Indianapolis

You can't fool us, Miss Victory, queening it
over the roofs of this city, one hip swishing
toward the long sword you cock
like a walking-stick between your calves.

Girlfriend, who welded that eagle to your scalp
and posed you with the liberty torch
like some bridesmaid's lucky catch?
Miss Victory, why, you're a certified virgin of war.

Your waist isn't wasp, there's no rumble-seat
festooning your behind. In the lingo of the parlor,
not the brawl, you remind us how we pussywhipped
the South. Are you trying to start something?

Your pectorals are rippling through your dress
and you've squared your Julius Caesar jaw.
To those shoppers down below
you're just a mannequin of camp.

No blood stipples your bronze bodice,
the polished cones of your breasts. Truth is,
you make war a costume drama, a tease,
your left hand flaming, the other hugging the hilt.

Nixon's Briefcase by Joseph Cornell

Nixon rubs his palm across the large pores
of the cordovan. For years, the smell and stroking
of leather have relaxed him. When he can't sleep,
he takes the satchel and imagines himself
on a palomino outside Muleshoe, Texas, or Wichita, Kansas.

Dreamily, he snaps open the case. The inside
is papered with the oily silver of newsprint,
an odor both solace and nemesis. Lining
the rim is a slender ribbon of tape.
Nixon makes sure that all is in place:

the world Tocqueville once imagined,
a compass, a clothes-brush, a clean shirt
and change of socks, canned sardines branded
with the portrait of a Danish king, an oval
Norelco shaver with rotating heads.

Nixon had wanted the inscription *Tempus fugit*
painted large inside. But instead the artist added a look
over the shoulder, a poisoned kiss. He decorated the clasp
with a curse. So when Nixon opens his briefcase
he feels like a pharaoh at the mouth of his own tomb.

Illinois

Shaped like Lincoln's face, veined red and blue,
the roadmap hovered, worn, above his bed.

While he sliced pears, steeped jasmine tea,
his Illinois took me in, deduced I was too new,

an immigrant unfamiliar with American moraines,
uncurious about Peoria or Cairo. But I touched

the tremulous state highways painted blue,
the branching Ohio River–beard, as his knife

glided into the swollen fruit. And when he appeared
with teapot and plate, the map slackened in the steam,

its borders wallowing in current and wave.
To him, Illinois meant home, Union terrain

his great-grandfathers fought for,
the alchemy of landscape into myth.

To me it was just a shape, landlocked and wet.
I gripped his muddy shoulders, his carp

and cottonmouth, the submerged willow root
I could wreck my life on.

Checkers

O my master of the armchair and the ottoman,
too frequently you baptize yourself in the long tub—
why not remain in the dirt like a truffle or a taproot?

For you, too, are powered by the soil, a hybrid of bulb
and brooding. In the dark, I devour your slippers:
narrow trenches of leather lined with ripe, damp fur.

Nixon and Nikita in the Kitchen

Moscow, 1959

At the threshold of the model American home,
Nikita accepts Nixon's arm. He had expected
a hostile man, an ugly one, but he finds Nixon
diminutive and charming. Together they test the springs
of the upholstered couch, exchange glances
over an episode of *Cheyenne*. Then Nikita allows himself

to be led to the tiny, tiled kitchen, where a pitcher
of martinis sweats on the counter. He forgets
to listen to the interpreter's discreet droning,
so intent is he on Nixon's calisthenic display:
here a rotisserie with its lazy spinning roast,
there a silver coffeepot in the shape of Sputnik,

and look, a big fridge that reminds him of the stables
of his childhood. Even the butter has its own berth,
its own little manger of glass. And that, he realizes,
is precisely Nixon's point: that in America, a man
derives joy from filling his automobile with fuel,
from coming home to a kitchen just like this

and watching the moon rise through his curtains.
Nikita wants to sing the praises of communal picnics
at mid-day in the wheatfields, where three hundred people
buzz over sandwiches of butter and meat.
But how can he persuade this slender American,
this shy stranger who probably has never laughed at a party,

except when a camera was pointed his way?
Nikita waves his arms but no sound comes out.
He imagines Nixon late at night, lonely under a circle
of kitchen light, with a wife and the appliances
spinning in the background. He sees Nixon
hunched over a pink teacup, blowing on his fingers,

afraid of everything he can't admit he fears.
Lev Tolstoy had it right, he thinks: *It is difficult
to tell the truth, and the young are rarely capable of it.*

II
Mastery

Learning to Draw

Leonardo! I'm learning to see
in fractions: the body in eighths,
the face in quarters, under the heavens
we are geometrical. Tomorrow
I will speak Chinese, spend the slowness
of the morning watching two glass jars
until my face feels like a prism. I

will be precise: sky, water, the wings
of the birds I hate
will no longer be blue but jay;
the walls not white
but eggshell or tusk. Warm colors
creep up close, cool ones stand aloof.

That is why the sky keeps its distance,
says Pavel, my teacher. In his language
sky and heaven are the same word.
Not here in the rust belt. Orange sky,
burning rivers, the art god in the streets
smiling on taxicabs and colas.

Not all roads lead to Florence or China.
My hand swerves on the intricate
rose of the compass. I will never
be ancient, but my teacups will sit
in their saucers, and my frogs any moment
will leap off the page.

Mastery

At 22, I snuck up on Rembrandt's pose
of middle age, the yes and no of it,
his funky brown doublet twisted from the light,
his burgher's face tipped toward it,
shrewd, assured, framed with a flat velvet cap,
a teardrop pearl threading his ear.

In those days, I craved blood oranges,
which my old man stole for me by the bag.
We had a 70s mirror from Goodwill,
stenciled with a brass sunset in one corner,
and a parrot named Jupiter. I loved
looking at myself. I have eloquent eyebrows.

So I decided to paint the Old Master
a parody that would sing like Barry Gibb
and sweat like a Tequila Sunrise:
I angled my face like Rembrandt's
against a postcard green, streaked
some sheer pink along the knife of my throat.

Six months gone then, I painted
my torso in a blue-black shawl,
like a judge's robe. My lips are pressed
tight, like I'd just sentenced a horse thief
to hang. My eyes (always the hard part)
look jellied like the eyes of the blind.

My sister wants to see this picture.
It's stacked among some canvases
behind a bag of kitty litter above the Kenmore.
During my six-year sabbatical from the family,
I missed Karen and her loquacious critiques.
But I still wish she liked my abstract stuff.

Now she's turned up her nose
at my gift of a monoprint. She wants
the "Rembrandt," believing it some transcript
of what was lost: a rescue or refuge.

WCW on Marsden Hartley

He's a querulous bit of baggage
　　　　more mineral than animal
　　　　　　　big as a limestone cliff

and as briny He stinks
　　　　of months without sex
　　　　　　　Over the bed a small tintype

Paris, the Quatres Arts Ball, 1912:
　　　　In turban and garlands of jade
　　　　　　　he was the new Tiresias

a watery love sheik with civet eyes
　　　　and nose like a wedge of marble
　　　　　　　I can't stand men who dress

as women he said then
　　　　nose quivering hips womanly
　　　　　　　And wouldn't you know

in the next room
　　　　a plaster sheet away
　　　　　　　we hear it gathering

momentum an unmistakable
　　　　creaking hand over mouth
　　　　　　　tooth on hand

They are newlyweds careless
　　　　around neighbors ignorant
　　　　　　　about plaster He gives me

a Gauloise scoots closer
　　　　but I too refuse him
　　　　　　　There is pigment

under his nails
  Bill he says *Bill!*
    And you would have made

the most charming whore
  in New York

Einstein's Train

The truth about our childhoods is stored up in our bodies. . . .

—*Alice Miller*

For years I will track you, tunnel
into your sleep, meet you coming
and going. Those of you who fear
loneliness, you will meet me only at death
before the swift unspooling. Better you,
the mute, the solitary, who, still alive, can learn
to travel both ways at once. Heraclitus lied:
You can step twice in the same river.
But only the second time will you feel
the yank of the current, your body
fighting to stay warm.

Only the second time will you smell her
Shalimar, feel her bending over you in the basement
under an absurd holy card of an angel
sweating on the painted concrete blocks.
Why did you remember the glass milk jugs,
the suntan hosiery overhead, but not this?
Because only now are you ready to unribbon
the Möbius strip of your heart, now that you hate enough,
now that you sleep between two mirrors
and let lightning strike you twice.

Revising Sylvia

May [Swenson] in the other room:
freckled, in herself, a tough little nut.
I imagined the situation of two lesbians:
the one winning a woman with child
from an apparently happy marriage.

Independent, self-possessed M.S. Ageless.
Bird-watching before breakfast. . . . My old
admiration for the strong, if lesbian, woman.
    — *Sylvia Plath, two journal entries,*
        Yaddo, November 1959

Eight-millimeter woman, phosphoric semaphore
of hands and hair spilling through the projector,
caftaned in light, rewind
this sheet, this film
now spooling through the projector,
rewind and splice the life that could have been:

now in your sixties, alive
against a Jugendstil window of Sappho
leaded with pomegranate and grape,
a rich pumpkin soup buttering your lip,
the beach a field of pepper,
white shade, black light
return, return

to Yaddo, leave a hasty note on Ted's pillow
like a bitter mint for him to suck
on his return to the whitewashed studio, the closet
gaping its inaudible white cadence,
your wellingtons in the trunk of a woman
whose fingers will fatten you with poems

Eight-millimeter woman, four months pregnant,
swelling as the earth shrivels in the frost,
run with your belly full of daughter
and your parcel of carbons
Flee with the woman who will drive you
beyond this vanishing point

now blurred as the elusive messenger
who hovers, wavers
but refuses to descend

Käthe Kollwitz, after a Visit to the New Russia, 1927

My model sleeps. But no matter—
the body slumped is a poem too.
Calloused hands open into petals.
The smudge between her lips
softens to an oval. Her neck
the color of bread and potatoes.

As a girl I probed for the ribs
under the skin of cats. Could I
have become a surgeon? Instead,
I put paper between me
and the body. Bones appeared.
Flesh. The freckled arm of a woman.
Her fingers closing the eyes
on her husband's swollen face.

Now I am old. I bend over this work
like a heavy bird. I breathe
with my eyes, praying for the star
to rise out of nowhere. In Moscow
I watched the rags on women's feet.
Even there hunger rattles on
like an empty train.

During the Sorties over Baghdad

A woman works with lace panels.
    Under and under again: that is the beauty
        of French seams. First to flatten with steam

back and forth back and forth.
    Then to stitch the unwavering rows
        the perfect parallels, all measures metric

all precise. To pinpoint the trajectory
    to plant the staccato thread under and under.
        This is the music of a thousand nights:

curtains scattered with trellises and roses
    scalloped along the valance and edges.
        Curtains fit for a window without flaw:

eight glass polygons, caulked, soldered
    fringed with the January frost, overlooking
        a city that has never been bombed.

Cleveland, Ohio, 1991

Shortwave

Warsaw, 1986

From Moscow, London, and Tripoli
shortwaves winged through the steel V

of our open antenna arms. Shrill dip of a calliope,
your hand on the tuner, then suddenly

the chimes of Big Ben, or a Russian
intoning his acquired English like a Californian,

the voice orbiting us beyond the thwack of beaten
rugs, our neighbors' telephones, a violin.

Black-shouldered and square, storied
as a bomber's briefcase, this Grundig 840,

assembled from Czech beer and Cuban lemons,
BBC'ed us kisses of astringent cadence

while we wrung underwear, typed letters,
scraped plates clean after supper.

In January, we slept in sweatpants
and mittens, your warm breath making my hair dance:

for days we lay curled together like an enormous ear
attending to concerts, quiz shows, propaganda, war.

As My Husband Translates from the Polish

Unselfconscious as a statue,
he sits heavily on a thin green chair,
the dusky bunch of genitalia
hanging between his open thighs.

He scowls, exasperated with lovers
he never met, with the spattered
imagery of cavalry and tanks.

He translates poetry in the nude,
in the raw—the pages around his feet
cast off like last night's clothes,
his lips silently moving

in love or in despair
at the hour
of someone else's death.

Babel

Scum from the pickle crock, dumplings with plum,
the Slovak uncles tossing old Stephen to the ceiling,
while the American daddy I thought was so smart
shrieked *dobry, dobry,* like a dim bird
from Bratislava, and Babcia flapped
her veined, impatient hands at him.
Linda pinched my arm for calling her "Dilna."
Sticks and stones, our mother said,
pinning a circle of lace to her scalp
as we climbed into cars for the Mass of St. Stephen.
Sweating like a calf in his purple dress,
the priest hummed high rising hymns
in a dead tongue, which the sad adults
echoed like children. Then all glided up
to the Communion rail, Grandpa
with his hat at his waist like a soldier—
he once wanted our mother to *scram*
but he said *scream* and when she did,
he taught her a lesson with a maple branch—
our mother who'd said *words will never hurt you.*
That winter night when she tucked me
under the *pierzyna* packed with feathers,
she sang about a silver horse with wings.

Dust Devils

Today, on the thirtieth day of the drought,
my bladder feels like a uterus—
swollen, straining, a yellow fist
unrelieved even by cranberry juice.
At every second gas station on I-80, I stop
to twist out a couple drops, feeling as impotent
as the monster birds of the Eocene
who, seven feet tall and wingless,
were all powerful till swift carnivores evolved.

I know how it feels to be cornered,
to be faced with old debts, to recognize
the end of an era. I see it in my sister-in-law
who throws a tantrum after stepping on her son's toy
triceratops. She has done the woman's thing all day—
dispensed cough medicine, changed crappy pants—
while her husband, a good-natured bison of a man,
laughs at her harried vigilance. I see it
in this year's corn, withering without silk
in penance for the trees replaced. I see it
in myself, the membranes of my body feverish
with the knowledge that I am what I produce, and lately

I can't even piss right. I wonder if
Dorothea Lange, that brave woman with her eye
to the viewfinder, ever shivered on the clay
floor of a sod house, her bladder steeped
in bacterial emulsion. Did she fear
implosion, the dry cyclone within? Did she feel
she was Kansas itself, all alkaline flats
and dust devils, hot wind and sod, the gray scale
between black and white?

III
Feast and Famine

Hermann Kafka's Dinnertime Pantoum

When Father says it's time, it's time!
Come, the table is for eating, not for chatter.
Why the long face, my skeleton-son?
It's jellied carp—my favorite!

The table is for eating, not for chatter—
Our dear cook has prepared us a feast.
It's jellied carp—my favorite!
Now, don't crack the bones with your teeth.

Our dear cook has prepared us a feast,
But sip the vinegar, please, without slurping
And don't crack the bones with your teeth.
Manners, for a Kafka, are everything.

Franz, sip the vinegar, please, without slurping
And take care not to scatter any scraps.
Manners, for a Kafka, are everything.
When I was a boy I wasted nothing

And took care not to scatter any scraps.
But, son, must you eat like a shadow?
When I was a boy I wasted nothing,
Never once did I languish on the sofa.

Son, must you eat like a shadow?
You are slow in all but the will to marry.
Never once did I languish on the sofa
Dreaming of love and grievances.

You are slow in all but the will to marry:
She parades before you in a lacy blouse,
Dreaming of love and grievances,
And right off you decide to marry her!

She parades before you in a lacy blouse,
Smiling, quoting your silly stories,
And right off you decide to marry her—
Will you never grow up?

Smiling, quoting your silly stories,
You're always scribbling in that notebook.
Will you never grow up?
A man needs manly work to be content.

You're always scribbling in that notebook—
Why the long face, my skeleton-son?
A man needs manly work to be content
And when Father says it's time, it's time!

Losing Language

It's Pan Zbyszek's funeral, and I'm running late.
I go with stumps of mushrooms slung
on a string, tongue stained red from currants.
Lateness, Zbyszek's niece has warned,
is the habit of cuckolds and tramps.

Melancholy veils the lindens, seeps
into the altar cloth's embroidered lamb,
melancholy will leaven the host,
bloody the wine in the chalice.
Basia tells of Zbyszek in his overcoat,
how he slumped in the snow on Jerusalem Street
after a supper of hunter's stew.

Perhaps this will be the night
when my tongue suddenly goes still.
Talk, though a pleasure, has come to seem
the folly of the brash,
a gift box too quickly opened
or the visage of a widow
stripped of her black Cracovian lace.

When Zbyszek's niece leads me to the pew
garlanded with the purple of regret,
I will not even hum the hymns.
For once, my mouth and body
will aspire to the key of silence.
When the soprano starts, I will not turn to gape
at the choir loft. When the spirit singes my forehead,
I will neither fidget nor flinch.

Making Pierogi

The dough is not turning out. It refuses
to stretch, sticks to the sides of the pink bowl.
You work in another half scoop of flour,
click your tongue, stamp your slippered foot.
And the flutter in my stomach quickens:
instinctive response to your anger, thrum
of guilt, *my fault*. In this room, once
dove gray, attic gold, brushed peach,
you presided in alligator flats,
though you could have been on stilts,
so tall you towered over us. You wanted
the gold-flecked linoleum to gleam,
the turquoise wool coat of your design
to disguise my sloping back, every plate
to be safe in its nesting place.
                              You are smaller now,
more comic, a banner of unbleached flour
on your belly pressed against the table edge
as you thump the rolling pin over the dough's
thin skin. My own body feels bigger,
too big for the braided mat of this chair,
flushed with the insight that you have become
my serious gray-haired girl. How stubbornly
you hold your shoulders, your pastry wheel
flaying the flat expanse of dough into strips.
Flour on my fingers, I crimp your tiny pillows
of plum and cheese, watch them bob
and float in the salty water, and rescue them
again and again.

Beyond the Velvet Curtain

Monthly I have come to these sands, monthly I have braved the
    surge,
waited to be buffed to a dull carnelian. Then the roast drips in its pan,

and the blood widow comes in her black mantilla, the spider whose
    twin spinnerets
wilt like carnations. Not for me to cast these heels into meathooks,

to wail on a sterile table and pass crap and blood, while a man in a
    miner's hat
aims his torch at my tunnels. I would rather lie flat as a holy card,

I would rather shimmer in a monstrance of my own making,
    untroubled
by suckling or swelling, than venture beyond that velvet curtain.

At 38, I could still cast aside the drape, let the dramaturge tug my
    ropes.
I could still be all the world, my own Shakespearean globe,
    commanding

the props of tenderness and rage. The poems I once killed for
would drip down my walls. But beyond the velvet curtain,

my mother waits. She loathes the hands patting her belly,
the metaphors of yeast and salt. I have seen her wax and wane, heard
    her keen

like a mink snagged by steel jaws. O Jesus Mary Joseph, O Catherine
    broken on the wheel:
pilot this empty gondola, this navigable slipper, beyond the slap, the
    first lungswell and shriek.

Drought

After the grass burned, after our great
lake lost three feet, after the dust
made your eyelids swell and we played
a tape of the tide rolling in
to remind us, after the blood soaked
through towel, sheet and mattress
and I returned from the clinic, sanitized
and sore, after you licked the gash between my legs
like a mammal grooming his dead young, after the hair
prickled up on my belly and I tethered your long face
in my thighs so as not to
lose it too, only then the water
came, your lips on my lips, my hands
in your hair, death
and the banishment of death, wave
after wave

Tureen

Through the lid-hole cut for a ladle
I smell onions and broccoli
breathing.

You who were the enemy
are offering me soup.

Two bowls, two spoons,
long branches floating
in flat green ponds.

Although the house belongs to you now,
I rise for knives and forks.
The thick stalks succumb
to mild sawing.

You push your bowl away.
"I can't do anything right."
And then you sob like a boy,
hiding your face, your shoulders
lifting and shuddering.

All my pet names for you
come to mind:
"Love-sheep," "lizard,"
"the big peach."

I want to kiss your hair,
float you in the tureen
of my arms
until the surface of your grief
stills.

Instead I reach for your plaid
flannel shoulder

like a teammate, perhaps a coach.
I hold you with a loose grip, one-handed,
to keep from slipping.

Sapphic Sonnets

J

Why do I try to gild you in this form?
I'd rather see you off the page and out
in Lake Monroe, pink otter with sleek arms
awash in dreamy waves, your eyes shut tight
or blinking three times fast like Shelley Winters
when you played Mrs. Malaprop from Minsk—
a slurper of oolong, devotee of banter,
who gargled her vowels, filched a neighbor's blintz—
Chekhovian, your sudden floods of tears!
You felt unlovable, painted your lips red,
I was too married to be your suitor,
but when I saw your diaphragm by the bed
(proof positive) I couldn't speak or look
too long at you: I felt forsaken back.

Z

"I could drink a case of you," you sang,
"and still I'd be on my feet, I would still
be on . . . my . . . feet." I loved the rich meringue
of your chanteuse routine, the swoop and growl
of it, batik knotted around your hips,
your neck arched back in a Ladino wail,
guitar on your belly, your handsome lips
engorged with grief, the audience in your spell.
By twenty, you had slept with thirteen men
and I, not one. You draped me in your stoles,
taught me to flirt, to dance, to cook with mint,
daubed wine on my earlobes, cologne on my heels.
And when your Catholic belle enjoyed success
you lavished her with matzos and a kiss.

S

Your fists were furious in Berlin, you cried
outside the phone booth in a rage. I felt
above your fit, a sheepish passerby,
while you waged on, triumphantly at fault.
Your flat was cold: two lemons in a bowl,
the windows scrubbed with vinegar, a small
Picasso's Stein that made me wonder if . . .
In bed (a narrow couch), I breathed a whiff
of rosemary from your tub: cool medicine,
sly trick that made me want to lick your knees,
to soap the thighs you hated, the never-thin
calves, even tease your stubby tantrum toes.
Instead, I twisted in the bleached, starched sheets,
my belly tense, my fingers awkward mates.

M

Come here, my frazzled girl giraffe. I'll weave
my hands into a vee, fidget your tight
trapezius, slip all your knots. You're brave
to surrender your spine, girl, to these mitts,
these clumsy ducks, which cling to handlebars,
while you ride cool, your arms above your head,
my macho queen, disdainful of my fears
on bikes and off. Together in my bed
we're chaste as saints, I in my Kafka shirt,
you in your floral gown, a pillow tucked
between your knees, unlike the dancehall flirt
you've been with other gals—I've seen your look—
the bolo ties, the way you swung them fast
while wishing someone would swing you, at last.

Frost Heaves

when the winter retches so hard the roads contort,
frost heaves when she shrugs off
even my hug of comfort; frost heaves
when she lets me brush the back of her neck
or leave a circle of thaw
with my mouth; frost heaves
like a Renaissance lyric
protesting the lady's coldness;
frost heaves when I touch myself
pretending to touch her

The Art of Love

I learned in my mother's kitchen, at her hands,
how to whip egg whites cleanly in a bowl,
till they billowed up like a ballerina's skirt,
then dropped like a curtsy on the pie.
I loved to scrape the skin from Jonathans
in curling strips and watch buds of chocolate
sweat saucily, dissolve to glossy waves,
while she supervised, gave orders, held me
to her standards. That's why I prefer it
alone now, no hand on the knife but mine,
my eye sole mistress of delight as I
melt and simmer my way to our repast.
Such priestly offices, chaste discipline!
Sweetheart, I don't want you to watch. You're not
of this order. I, too, have hung around
kitchens of former loves, watching Frank
chop cilantro and chiles, Michael shape
croissants. Like you, I too tried to steal sips,
beg hugs, slip my hand under a belt, but
preoccupied, they bristled with reproof.
Just wait. After I steam the rice, reduce
the sauce, sauté the chicken with tarragon
and grapes, after I watch every morsel
disappear, then, satisfied that you are
satisfied, I'll let you lay hands on me.

Wedding Song

Jankowice, Poland, 1986

I do what I can for Hanka, daughter
of my wife, even though her heavy
pregnant breasts remind me of yours,
Natalia, you wicked collector of silver
earrings and the thick, veined poles
of our cocks. In the last pew I see

your flagrant, skillful hands on the hymnal,
your showy gold teeth and fringed
shawl with poppies. You pretend
to be demure: how else to coax
us pickle-noses under the striped
wool awning of your skirt? Ah Natalia,

even though I have broken in a new wife—
a good worker who carts arm-loads of beets
on her bicycle, an angel who soothes the bruised
skin under my eyes when I'm sad—I miss
your rouged Cleopatra lips, your lovely
nylon thighs. What I never gave you

Hanka the bride shall have: three hogs,
a hundred flasks of vodka, a four-man band
to wheeze out polkas and waltzes all week.
Her groom is a handsome fool like I was.
He parades like the Lord at Cana, though it is I
who have paid for the music and the feast.

Oh Natalia, my wife refuses to invite you
so I will ask the American niece to dance.
I will gallop her over this hollow floor
in tight, dizzy rings till her breasts
bloom like apples, silver hoops
appear in her ears and she stares up at me

loving and hard, the shoes flying from her feet,
dinner plates breaking, the windows blowing out,
every hound in this village baying and howling,
the pale eagle of Poland sweeping off its crest,
our stamping and whirring heard
as far as the silver moon itself.

IV
Exile

Saint Elizabeth, Queen of Hungary

Nights, under the tasseled brocade of my canopy
I can see them, taut with hunger, eyes

overly large and glittering. The chambermaids
dab at my hairline with tiny linen cloths,

murmur something about sheep. Fools!
My flock is more than my husband.

There is no peace here. I can't sleep.
I will fill my shawl with bread, slip out

to the street. If guards block me, I will shower them
with roses big as dinner rolls, gaudy as the blood

of Our Lord. If they don't I will open my shawl
to you. I will hold your hungry bones in my arms.

Feast. No man can live without it.

Watching My Father Pray

We are no longer in Europe, in his father's provincial town
named for the warring saint who split his cloak with a sword
to shelter a strange man. We are twice removed from the women
in black crochet, keening the rosary in chorus to send off
the dreaming dead in narrow boats of spun sugar.

Here prayer occurs in the bedroom, silent as sex, his eyes closed,
hands bunched below his waist. He looks awkward
in his tee shirt and boxers, a boy too big to be on his knees.

If only we were a people who shook our fists. If only we prayed
with our arms open to summon music, embrace a passionate God.
Instead, our prayers always take the same form: *Father, let me not pass
from this world unloved.* All our lives like this, Dad.
All the hours on our knees, praying for the wrong thing.

What My Father Taught Me About Sex

That my mother and he never "had relations"
before the wedding, that even now when she sits on his lap
he squirms, turns red and tells her she's fat
as she kisses his neck and pretends he's Clark Gable.
Yet he loves to move her around the dance floor,
his left palm tucked into the trough of her back.

That I should play poker instead, or read a book,
that I shouldn't give away the milk for free, for who would want
the cow, that I should wait till I marry and if I never marry
to keep myself chaste as a saint, to cultivate vegetables
or a musical life, to touch only the skin
of the piano, for he had always wanted to play.

Cuba Libre

The plywood bar in the basement
glistened with silverfish,
teardrop heads jerking
in wet veins of wood.
An Emerson radio, amber
from overuse, erupted
in sudden bursts of static.
I'd never been left alone before.
The armrests of my vinyl chair
felt slick with dew or mildew.
I squeezed my eyes tight.

When I opened them again,
I saw *Life*, October '62,
on the blonde endtable.
The black cover blared:
Is God Dead?
Dumb question. I knew about Easter,
the angel rolling away the stone,
Jesus, in shining "garments"
rising like a lily from the grave.

I smoothed the long, slick cover,
pried apart the sticky pages.
There was a basement, stocked
with canned corn and soup,
glass jugs of water.
—"If you love your children,"
the caption said, "bombproof your home."
Once Dad and Uncle Stevie
had argued about war:
would the Russians and Castro
bomb Chicago? *Bomb*,
they said, *bomb . . . bomb*
—a cartoon noise without pictures.

An orange box of *Tide*
glowed like a bulls-eye and bled
through to the next page
onto the suit of the First Lady,
Jackie, who wore heels and smiled
like my first-grade teacher.
They were all happy—kids cradling
the hi-fi, the lady in a long brassiere.
Brazier, I guessed, *brassier*.
I felt like I never felt
when reading *Yertle the Turtle*—
sad, dizzy, as if someone
had told me half a secret
more scary than the scuttling silverfish,
the mildewed brown linoleum
buckling like a recent grave.

A key scraped the lock:
Mom back from Van Til's.
Hello, she called, *Anyone home?*
It was October 1962,
in East Chicago, Indiana,
and the ring of milk bottles,
soft click of the fridge,
already sounded like the past.
I wanted to remain in the future,
slicing apart the pages, beyond
the primer of Mother's muted heels
popping and sparking up above.

Polish Jokes

In the deep freeze of the cold war,
we wanted to defect from the punchlines
about garbage trucks and light bulbs.
Pete wished to be Irish, to roll rainbow
slices of corned beef on his tongue
and sing in green parades. Irene envied the verve
of the French, their eloquent shrugging and escargots.
Uncle Ray changed the family name
to Kramer, married a sorority WASP,
then disappeared down a gimlet glass
into the carpeted gullet of IBM.

I, however, preferred my treachery private.
Only the absorbent towels, the dirty tongues
of linoleum in my parents' bath
ever saw me repudiate my heritage.
Only the shower curtain, the one-eyed lady
on the bath-size bar of Camay
spied me naked, touching a frigid
juice glass to my lips, breathing caresses
in Swedish. Only the Kleenex box,
my father's squat hairbrush witnessed
the room filling up with steam,
a Stockholm of my own
for feigning détente while dreaming of exile.

Lawrence Welk

I loved my Gram, but couldn't stand her show—
the matching purple coffins for the band,
six feet of bubbles, Larry's tiny wand
that cued the strings above, the brass below.
A patriarch who wouldn't be told "No,"
he coaxed the Lennon girls to dip and bend,
adjusted Sissy's bra strap with gloved hand,
and tamed trombone, cornet, and piccolo.
But Gram preferred to take another view:
when Lawrence asked the audience to dance,
ladies with bouffant hair and sequined shoes,
she moved close to the screen in shy suspense
as if the man whose accent was like hers
would polka *her* around the universe.

Synecdoche

Curious the mute relics you left me—
blunt pencils from the Paducah Bank,
Celtic candles that weep thick green tears on the tablecloth—
which I examine as if something animate,
something that could make you
blink or stare or blush might come
from holding what you held.

Yes, now begins the unholy idolatry,
the fixed images I haul from town to town.
Believe me, I am crafty and medieval,
what I have of you is dear:
here your holy finger, there the aura of your beard,
the moon-shaped scar on your knee
that swears you are flesh.

If only we were only our bodies,
our tongues locking worshipfully
in each other's grooves.
Or if we were more like my landlord, Jack,
sinking his careful, platonic putts
in the clipped green rug
of the basement floor.

Instead, I am living in the Church of the Assumption
of my childhood—its French provincial turrets and cupolas,
the conventional plaster poses of its apostles
approximating the Kingdom of Heaven.
Is it absurd to hold out for the true communion of saints,
the great yawning resurrection of the dead?
And if not, how to burnish in imagination
lips, eyes, beard, talk, hands
without consuming or freezing the kingdom?

Exile

O marble aunts and grandparents
planted in this alien soil
you are clay now, like bedrock
gods to me. You appear as in life, teeth loose,

slack aprons over the dangling
plums of your breasts, speaking in the singsong
Carpathian cadence of childhood.
I pat geraniums into place

over your folded arms, light candles,
and for this penance of spade and pick
ask you to absolve me of the children
I have neglected to bear, the husband

I grind my teeth at in the night.
I am uncertain as you were before the passage,
wary at the new world awaiting.
The car is packed to bursting:

I am leaving you. But I will plant
shrines. I will take with me your missing
teeth, your sweaty blankets, the food
and sex of more lifetimes than this.

You will live on like most exquisite smelly saints
at the tips of my fingers, in the moss
between my thighs, like candles at my throat,
fat lilies in my arms and growing hair.

Come as You Are

She drives all night through the bovine dark,
drinking pop from the can, fumbling for change
to feed the insatiable booths, their bellies of mesh.
Red light, green light: *Pay Toll! Thank You!*
How did she end up this desperate
for familiarity, the sound of someone else's
breathing in sleep? Surely, she thinks,
we were not meant to live alone.

Her ancestors, who herded sheep
in the High Tatras, lived three generations
to a house. They had, if nothing else, dull uncles
to annoy. Living alone is too polite,
too Romantic. She feels like the Rousseau
of house pets and aggressive ferns. While suppering
on chicken from a jar, brussel sprouts
from a box, she has time to get anxious about

all those things the herd dwellers don't,
not the least of which is dying alone.
It's easy to feel immortal at a Cubs game,
or in her friend's kitchen strung with oregano
and chiles, or in her lover's bed
when she hears the sea in his ears.
Not so, alone. She hears what eternity
will sound like: quiet

but for the sometime swoosh of cars.
Quiet has become so much the habit
that when she finally arrives, when he pulls back
the blanket to make room, when she smells his hair, hears
the hoarse morningness of his voice, she feels
shivery as a veal calf suddenly sprung
from his narrow box. How to live in this unexpected
abundance? How, later, to fit back in the box?

Notes

The extended metaphor in "Citoyen" was suggested to me by an unforgettable gesture in Andrzej Wajda's film *Danton*, in which Robespierre is summoned to a private and very sumptuous banquet at the mansion of Danton, who fills a goblet to the brim and invites his guest to drink. Robespierre, the epitome of control, downs the glass without spilling.

"Breslau" grew out of a personal loss I suffered and also out of a fascination with the Polish city Wrocław (previously Breslau), which had been 90 percent destroyed during the war and had lost all traces of Germanness except for yellowing family bibles in the antiquarian bookstores and tram tracks that went nowhere in the city center. It was a great propaganda point with the Polish People's Republic that Wrocław was and always had been a Polish city. Walking the streets there, I sometimes imagined myself in a city layered like Troy.

The thirty-foot bronze "Miss Victory" stands atop the Soldiers and Sailors Monument in downtown Indianapolis. The monument commissioners in 1895 described the statue, which had been designed by George Brewster of Cleveland, as follows: "Her right hand holds a sword, the point of which rests on the globe, and symbolizes the army to which victory was due, while in her left hand she holds aloft a torch, emblematic of the light of civilization. The young eagle perched lightly on her brow is typical of the freedom resulting from the triumph and light." For other examples of civic statuary featuring feminized icons of war, see Marina Warner's *Monuments and Maidens: The Allegory of the Female Form* (New York: Atheneum, 1985).

The American modernist painter Marsden Hartley (1877–1943) was associated with the Alfred Stieglitz circle, which also included Georgia O'Keeffe, Arthur Dove, and John Marin. Originally from Maine, Hartley is acknowledged to have done his best work late in life when, after years of wandering, he returned to his native region and painted primitivist landscapes and portraits. The dramatic situation for this poem comes from an excerpt of William Carlos Williams's *Autobiography* (New York: Random House, 1951), 172–73.

The poem about Käthe Kollwitz arose from an argument I had with my drawing teacher in Warsaw, a professor at the Fine Arts Academy (who considered Kollwitz "distinctly unmodern" and was scornful of her socialism), and from an obscure biographical note in *The Oxford Companion to Twentieth-Century Art*, ed. Harold Osborne (New York: Oxford University Press, 1981), 299–300.

For meteorological information about drought and dust devils, I'm indebted to Joseph E. Van Riper, *Man's Physical World*, 2d ed. (New York: McGraw-Hill, 1971), 233–35.

I'm indebted to Kafka's "Letter to His Father," in *The Sons*, translated by Ernst Kaiser and Eithne Wilkins (New York: Schocken Books, 1989), for some of the images in "Hermann Kafka's Dinnertime Pantoum."

In "Sapphic Sonnets" [Z], the chanteuse sings "A Case of You" by Joni Mitchell, which appeared on her album *Blue*, ©1971, Warner Bros. Records.

As children, my sister and I each had small, illustrated volumes of the lives of the saints. Saint Elizabeth was indeed a Hungarian queen who was supposed to have been devoted to the poor. According to the story I remember, the king, Elizabeth's husband, was embarrassed by his wife's charitable works and, for a time, forbade her to leave the castle. Once, as Elizabeth tried to sneak out with a cloak full of bread, the castle guards stopped her. Legend has it that when they slit open the cloak, roses rather than bread spilled out, and they allowed her to go on her way.